From Boys to Men

Mentoring Your Son for a Lifetime of Success

By Jay N. Rollins

For information about bulk copies and discounts for your organization, non-profit, or school, visit www.BoysToMenGuide.com

Printed in the United States of America.

First Printing, 2020

ISBN 9781652047452

JNR ENTERPRISES
3351 OAK ST.
WHEAT RIDGE, CO 80033
www.JayNRollins.com

Dedication & Acknowledgement

To my son, this inspiration for this book. You have become an incredible man with dreams and goals that make me proud.

To all those raising boys, you have an essential role to play, and it's an honor to be beside you for the ride.

"Success is the ability to control your own destiny, which provides for peace of mind."

Table of Contents

Preface

I am the product of a typical middle-class family. I went to public schools and attended a land-grant state university. My father was in new home sales, and my mother was a homemaker. Compared to some, I had advantages, and compared to others, I did not. However, at the time, I was not aware of these differences, so they did not matter.

From an early age, I had a passion for success, an entrepreneurial spirit. I sold Kool-Aid, shoveled snow, raked leaves, worked as a laborer on construction sites, and performed any additional odd jobs I could find to make a few dollars.

I enjoyed making money because it gave me freedom, and it made options available to me when I had money versus the times when I didn't. I was fascinated by the factors and characteristics that seemed to make some people financially successful and left others struggling. I also had the sobering experience of watching my father lose his job on multiple occasions and feeling the stress it put on the family.

My father was great. I loved him deeply. I watched him struggle, and it hurt as a young boy. I was around 16 years old when I watched him lose his job and send out resumes to find a new job. He lost his job in Detroit and moved the family to Washington DC. It was a good move, but again he was controlled by others to make money to support his family. That is one reason I chose to become an entrepreneur. I could control my own destiny, good or bad, whatever happened it was going to be based on my decisions and actions. I did not want others to control my life. My father never controlled his own destiny; other people did, and therefore they were controlling mine. This formed my initial view of success. For many people, that means a lot of money, which is fine, but it does not have too. It depends on the person.

I realized that no one was teaching me about success or talking about achievement and how to pursue success. Teachers only talked about getting good grades and getting a good job. To me, something was missing, and I went on a journey to find what that was.

This journey leads me to immerse myself in self-help, achievement, and success-oriented books. I was obsessed with understanding what made people successful and what success was. The problem was that by the time I knew enough to set out on this journey, I was already in my mid-20s and the middle of a banking career.

When I looked around the bank, it was clear that most successful people were not necessarily smart. The most successful people were the most likable, gregarious, and the best compensated. They were the relationship people who took the meetings, had lunches, and enjoyed afternoons of golf. These people were not the ones with the academic pedigrees, but they excelled at human relations.

Today I am the CEO of a growing real estate finance company I started over ten years ago based on what I learned over several decades. I employ the practices of goal-setting and recording my goals. I continue to observe what makes others successful and put to good effect all I have learned about human relations, achievement, and success. I am proud of what I have accomplished.

Before starting my own business, however, something else happened. I had a son. Like all parents, I wanted my child to have a better life than my own. As I relived the elementary school process through my son's experiences, and it became clear that, in regards to success and achievement training, nothing had changed in 30 years. No one at my son's schools talked about success techniques, the characteristics of a successful person, and how important goals are in shaping your life and getting what you want. Teachers, administrators, and curriculum all emphasized good grades, strong test scores, and connecting those to secure a good job. I rejected this narrative once again, but now I had to take action. I knew my son's future was at stake.

From the time my son turned eight years old, I started taking him on an annual retreat. Every Labor Day weekend, we would stay in a cabin in the mountains and talk about the traits that made people successful in life and happy as human beings, as well as the goal-setting necessary to achieve one's dreams and desires. People always say, *"you can be anything you want,"* but no one tells you how. I was determined to show him how.

This book culminated in ten years of retreats with my son and the research that guided them. It's intended to be an interactive manual for parents to use as a catalyst to talk to your sons about success, achievement, and goals. The worksheets are meant for parents to complete with your son. You won't find the information included here within any textbook at school. The topics are usually not discussed at the dinner table, yet the techniques and ideas presented can make the difference between a life well-lived (your son's definition of success as defined in the next section) or a life of mere survival.

I am pleased to say my son has turned out to be an exceptional young man with a set of "soft skills" I never had. Our time together has been an incredible journey; I am proud of who he is and cannot wait to see how he applies the knowledge we've built together in the next phases of his life.

It's my hope you will find this book, the activities it features, and the discussions it prompts as valuable as we have.

Good luck, and enjoy the journey!

Creating A Definition of Success

Through my self-education in success and my observations of others, I started to understand goals and goal-setting better. I discovered the power of writing down a thought or idea and how the simple act of putting a concept to paper made it real.

By this time, I was in my early 30s and witnessed the powerful ebbs and flows of corporate America. It seemed people could lose their income and self-worth in an instant due to an event such as a merger or recession, incidents entirely outside of their control. **It was then I began to understand real success was not about money, but about managing your destiny and taking measures to insulate yourself from events beyond your control.**

People are motivated by different things. Also, success is how others view you, your health - money cannot buy those things. Money may be a tool, but it's not the end game itself.

When I was a senior in college, I was soon to graduate with a degree in Finance. I didn't know what I would do with that degree, but college brainwashed me to aspire to work for a big company. The mantra was, get a job at a big company, and you'll be set. I didn't know any better.

IBM was interviewing on campus, and in the 1980s, no company was bigger and more prestigious than IBM.

I went through the on-campus process, and I was invited to come to their Washington DC location to do more interviewing there. I was so excited. I thought if I could get this one job, my future would be set forever. I bought a new suit, bought a new tie, and went to the interview. I thought I did well, but I went back to campus, not knowing the outcome.

As I waited to hear from them, I had two very different feelings.

1. If I get this job, I would be set for life. People's career at IBM was like the gold standard. All my fears could be put to rest.

2. It felt odd that one decision could be that impactful, and this company was controlling me somewhat.

I struggled with these two feelings.

Ultimately IBM called, and said they would not offer me the job. While I was disappointed, I also had a feeling of relief.

I could not put into words then, but I was about to hand over my destiny to someone else, and that did not feel good.

The two feelings I had were my inner struggle with the meaning of success. I did not know it then, but my definition of success was evolving. My interpretation was not to let anyone or anything control my destiny.

It was at that moment I knew I wanted more control over my life. At the time, I did not put that together with understanding the entrepreneurial lifestyle, but I did realize I wanted something where I could have more control. Controlling my destiny became the single most important thing in my career. I would go to make most of my career decisions around that principal. I wanted to succeed or fail on my terms, and I did not want to put my success in anyone else's hands.

That was my definition of success, and it does not have to be yours. The important thing is to be honest with yourself, know your definition of success, and understand what you are willing to sacrifice to get there.

Success for your son can be defined as:

- Your son has control of his destiny. Money helps, but if you're a screenplay writer and don't make a ton of money, but you're doing what you want and love, you have success.
- Your son is at peace and is not worried or scared. He has security and total peace of mind.
- Your son has options on how to spend his time.

If your son can achieve these things, that will be the ultimate success.

For some, that means having a lot of money. For others, it means adjusting their lifestyles to fit the money they have, but the goal is to eventually get out of the rat race and get off the treadmill, and be in control of your future.

But, how do you get there?

These are the key principles:

1. Knowing what you want
2. Having goals (so you can determine what you want)
3. Having action steps towards your goals
4. Holding yourself accountable to those goals
5. Without this, life will just happen, and you will not be in control of anything

It's never too early to start this process in teaching your son. It should start at least by the age of 10. I found it easier to create a format that he will understand, as it's about his life. Use these Big Six Life Categories to build your success foundation with your son.

The Big Six Life Categories

1. School
2. Sports/activities
3. Relationships
4. Hobbies/passions
5. Health
6. Job/career

How to Use This Book

This book was written with one goal in mind: to provide techniques and strategies to parents so they can coach and mentor their sons on how to set age-appropriate goals and ultimately be successful in life.

My goal for this book is to give you as parents the tools, structure and prompts needed to take your sons through a series of exercises that will get them thinking about their future at any age and setting goals that they can accomplish now to get there. These worksheets will start to help your young man begin to define success for himself.

For downloads and worksheets visit www.BoysToMenGuide.com

True success includes:

- Happiness
- Life options
- Freedom to pursue dreams and the confidence to achieve them
- Contentment and fulfillment
- Peace of mind
- Integrity
- Respect for oneself and respect for and from others

How do we obtain these things?

1) Have dreams (or a vision) for each part of your life (we call these dreams the Big Six Life Categories)
2) Have goals for each of your Big Six
3) Have an action plan around each goal
4) Execute that plan

These things are not taught in school. You will have to teach them to your son. This book seeks to make it easier by outlining a path to success.

This book is written in the form of a manual. I suggest, as a parent/son team, you use it as follows:

1. Go through the book together, allowing your son to answer as many questions as possible.
2. For any question(s) your son cannot answer, push him a bit. Keep asking questions.
3. Take 2–3 hours to review your son's answers. Ask your son why he chose to answer the questions the way he did.
4. Review your son's goals. Help your son to clarify his vision of success, and help your son develop his success by keeping goals in mind and working toward them each day.

If you help your son to work on updating action steps regularly and establishing new goals, he will develop tools to pursue a lifetime of success.

1. This book is broken down as follows:

   - Part I: Where You Are Now and Where You Want to Go
     - **Chapter 1: The Self-Assessment: Baseline – Where You Are Now**
       - Goal - To create an understanding of where you are now and where you would like to be in the future. These will allow you to measure growth toward your goals.

- Chapter 2: Success - What It Is & How to Get It
  - Goal - To understand success, the traits of successful people, and how to create your vision of success.

2. Establish actions and behaviors to get you to your dreams.
   - Part II: The Success Roadmap
     - **Chapter 3: Relationships**
       - Goal - To understand the importance of relationships and how they can help you achieve your goals.
     - **Chapter 4: Time Management**
       - Goal - To create a system to make the best use of your time.
     - **Chapter 5: Decision Making**
       - Goal - To understand the importance of decision making and to learn strategies for making the right decisions.
     - **Chapter 6: Success Techniques**
       - Goal - To remind you what will help you to achieve your dreams and what you should avoid.

3. Set up goals and tools to stick to your plans and work hard every day.
   - Part III: Your Ongoing Journey to Success
     - **Chapter 7: Setting Your Goals and Designing Your Life**
       - Goal: To create well-defined action-oriented goals to help meet your dreams for your life.

Together, these components lead the way to helping your son build a lifetime of success.

Part I

Where You Are Now
and Where You Want to Go

Success Is About Knowing What You Want

Most people complain about what they don't like, but they never stop and think about what they want. Knowing what you want is much harder than simply saying what you don't like. That is because it is easy to complain, but knowing what you want sounds final, and that's scary.

Don't be afraid. What you want can change, but knowing what you want is the key to establishing goals, and your goals are the keys to your success.

Success means very different things to us all. It's not all about money. Money is or maybe a byproduct of doing what you want.

When I was a young banker in the early 90s, I was meeting a lot of business people: some large company executives, some small business owners.

I was struggling to figure out as a young man where I would fit in. A large company, a small company, I did not know what I wanted, and it concerned me.

During that time, I had a homebuilding client, Bob Koury of Sunshine Homes. I knew Bob was financially successful because I saw his financial statements.

Bob ran a small home builder with about five employees in a 2,000 square foot office. When I would meet with Bob, he was always barefoot, in shorts and a Hawaiian shirt. Bob dressed how he wanted, he was doing what he wanted, and was making good money. He did not want to grow or be part of a big company. He just wanted to do what he was doing.

I thought to myself "Bob is the most successful person I know." I wanted to model myself after Bob Koury.

From that point on, I built a boutique business and shunned large businesses, knowing that small businesses could lead me to what I wanted.

Find your role model of success. See it on others, then model yourself after that. In doing so, you will begin to understand what you want.

The pathway to success is not as hard as you think. Success involves:

1) Knowing what you want
2) Having a vision for your life or dreams - being able to see in your mind what "victory" or success looks like
3) Having written goals and action steps and deadlines for each goal
4) Then continue to review and update your goals and make sure they continue to link back to your dreams

Once you have dreams or a vision for each part of your life and goals/action steps that get you closer to your dreams, you are on your way to achieving the success you want in parts of your life.

This book will prepare you for your success journey. It will:

- Help you understand where you are now.
- Establish a dream for each part of your life that is important to you (knowing what you want).
- Help you establish goals for each of your dreams.
- Provide tips to eliminate roadblocks along the way.
- Provide tips to help you move faster toward your goals.

When the book is completed, your son will have his Success Plan!

Now, let's get going. The self-assessment on the following pages will help your son realize where they are now and how they presently think about the future.

Chapter 1

The Self-Assessment:
Understanding What You Want

Baseline – Where You Are Now

Before we begin to dive into success techniques, let's start with a self-assessment.

Self-assessment is the first step to self-awareness. Analyzing strengths, weaknesses, and ambitions is essential in knowing yourself.

Consider the following prompts and write down what comes to mind for your son. There are no right or wrong answers. It is all about self-awareness, which is clarity. Without clarity, you can be lost and easily swayed by the crowd. Clarity is the start of the success process.

My son was clear on the fact that he wanted to play baseball. To do so, he would need to practice. Then he would have to try out to make the team. If he didn't make it, he would need to practice some more.

Creating a baseline is about the truth and honesty with yourself. You have to be your harshest critic, as others will not typically tell you things you do not want to hear.

As a parent, it's your job to give your son a baseline, even if it's not pleasant.

I remember when my son was playing competitive youth baseball. He did well at the 10/11-year-old level. He was one of the best players on the team. But this was before the boys went through puberty.

When the boys got to be 12 and 13, some of them grew and developed faster. My son did not. Because he was late in his growth, his strength and skills were not as good as the boys going through puberty.

I had to sit him down and give him a baseline talk. I told him the following:

- You're going to be late in developing (I was too), and it's going to affect your ability to compete for a while.

- You can either give up or work harder to keep up with the boys who are developing faster.

- If you want to compete, you will need to start a weight training and nutrition program. You are going to have to take extra reps and practice harder than others. You can complain and say it's not fair, but that is what it will take to reach your goals.

My son was disappointed to hear this, but he accepted it. Then he took it as a personal challenge and started a training and practice program. He kept up and was able to stay on the team.

These are all steps in the success journey. To have the clarity you must have self-awareness.

Your Son's Self-assessment (ask him to answer these questions)

1. Describe your strengths (what you think of as your best qualities):

2. Describe your weaknesses (areas you'd like to improve upon):

3. What things are important to you now? (List the things that matter most):

4. What things do you think will be important to you in the future (10 years from now):

5. List 10 things you'd like to accomplish in your life and circle the top five.

The next section of this book will show you how to help your son plan for his journey by solidifying his dreams for each segment of his life. He will then be ready to begin developing traits of successful people. They include the following:

- Strong relationships
- Effective time management
- Good decision making
- Progressive goal setting

Finally, you will help him:

- Learn multiple success techniques and how to avoid success killers
- Set up a personal Success Plan
- Keep the destination in mind with Mirror Goals

Your son's Success Plan and Mirror Goals will be the key written documents that will guide him on every step of his journey.

Chapter 2

Success – What It Is and How to Get It

Understanding What Success Means to You

Success did not come easy or fast for me, primarily because I did not know what I wanted. I worked at large banks and large homebuilders, and I struggled inside these larger institutions. I was not good at corporate politics. I did not do well with certain types of people, primarily lower performers. I resisted bureaucracy. I did not understand why I had these problems, and I did not know how to solve them.

In my late 20's, I went to work for a large home builder. I got politically sideways with a person with much more authority. I was not even sure how or why the argument began. The result was that I was laid off, or fired, or whatever you want to call it.

While I was upset, I also felt somewhat free.

Following this, I was forced to make some tough decisions and go a different route. I decided that I wanted to form my own business that would buy distressed real estate assets. I did not have the money to do it, so I called on one of my old banking clients, Gordon Smith. Gordon liked the idea, and we formed a business together.

I remember my first day. He gave me a 10x10 conference room, and we had two desks, metal file cabinets, two computers, and two phones. It was sparse, but it was mine, and I was in business. From then on, I knew whatever happened to me would be a result of what I did, and I would not be subject to the whims of others.

At that point, I had made very little money and the business had no revenues, but it was then that I genuinely felt successful. I was successful because I owned my destiny. That was a success to me, and that is what I continue to teach my son. If you control your future, you are successful.

What is success? Success is different for everyone. Most people think success is simply about money. But for many, success is not about money and maybe more personal. We all have to establish our own definition of success. What definition is best for you? For your son? You may find he is drawn to a few different definitions, which are okay, too.

Example Definitions of Success

- Consistent positive outcomes in all parts of life
- Control over your own destiny/life
- Choosing what you want to do, not what you have to do
- Gained respect of family, friends, and peers

A personal vision of success
Success starts with a vision or a dream. Vision is a dream of knowing what you want and being able to imagine yourself getting it, living it. You should have a clear vision for each part of your life.

1. Having a vision for each key part of your son's life will guide him each day, making his decision making easier and better.

2. **The Big Six Life Categories:** Everyone's life is different, and you will have other things that are important to you, but to start, we are providing you with the following "Big Six" components of your life. As your son gets older, his dreams for different parts of his life will change. However, six essential areas of his life will remain constant. They are:

    1. School
    2. Sports/activities
    3. Relationships
    4. Hobbies/passions
    5. Health
    6. Job/career

Here are some possible examples:

1) **School**:
Dream: Attend a college or university.
Goal: Get a 3.5-grade point average.
Action step: Study 2-3 hours every night

2) **Sports/Activities:**
Dream: Be a starter on the varsity basketball team.
Goal: Make 90% of my free throw shots
Action step: Practice on my shot for an hour each day

3) **Relationships:**
Dream: Have a supportive girlfriend.
Goal: Maintain open communication.
Action step: Spend time talking, not just texting

4) **Hobbies/Passions:**
Dream: Rebuild an old car
Goal: Learn how to rebuild an engine
Action step: Sign up for a mechanics class

5) **Health**:
Dream: Have excellent health and be fit.
Goal: Be able to bench press my body weight
Action step: Work out four times per week

6) **Job/Career**:
Dream: Own my own business
Goal: Be profitable in the first year
Action step: Decide on a business idea

Designing Your Life

Now let's help your son create a personal vision for each part of his life. Have him fill in the sections of the "Design Your Life" plan. These will help him figure out exactly what he wants and give him the clarity he needs to start making all of his dreams and goals a reality.

Have your son keep his dreams in mind as you both move forward. He will use them again in his Success Plan in Chapter 7.

Note: This is not easy. It takes time and thought.

1. Describe your life now. What is good, and what is not working so well?

2. Describe the life you want at the next level in your life - high school/college (i.e., grades, friends, sports, jobs, class, etc.).

3. Describe the life you want when you are 25 years old. Where are you working? Where are you living? Towards what are you working?

4. Describe the life you want when you are 35 years old. Are you married, do you have kids, where are you living, what is your career?

Now that you have helped your son create his vision and dream, let us now combine his dreams with the Big Six Life Categories.

Ask your son the following questions and have him fill out the answers below.

School:

1. What do you want to get out of school this year (grades, clubs, etc.)?

2. What does it take to achieve what you want at school?

3. What can you do every day to help yourself achieve what you want?

Sports/Activities:

1. What sports or activities are most important to you, and what do you want from these sports or activities?

2. What will it take to achieve what you want in these sports/activities?

3. What can you do every day to help yourself achieve what you want?

Relationships:

1.   What relationships are the most important to you?

2.   What does it take for you to create or improve these relationships?

3.   What can you do every day to create better relationships?

Hobbies/Passions:

1.   What are your favorite hobbies or passions?

2.   What does it take to achieve what you want for your hobbies or passions?

3.   What can you do every day to help yourself achieve your goals in your hobbies or passions?

Health:

1.   Is good health important to you? If yes, what does good health mean to you? How can you describe it?

2.   What will it take for you to have good health?

3.   What can you do every day to achieve "good health"?

Job/Career:

1.   What are some ideas around what you want to do/be when you grow up?

2.   How do you want to spend your days as an adult?

3.   Right now, what are some ways you can earn some money?

4.   What are some things you need money for now? What will it take for you to achieve your money goals?

5.   What can you do every day to make these goals a reality?

What is your vision of success for each of the Big Six Life Categories and any additional categories you have chosen?

1. School

2. Sport/Activities

3. Relationships

4. Hobbies/Passions

5. Health

6. Job/Career

The Traits of Successful People

It is essential to say that success is not about how much money you have. Often money follows success as a byproduct of someone being very good in their chosen field.

For example, J.K. Rowling became a successful author of a fantasy book series, Harry Potter, and money followed. But before Harry Potter, she was first successful in following her dream of writing, which led her to write a book that millions of people wanted to read.

Alternatively, many people never made it big, never made millions, but are truly successful because they lived the life they wanted to live. They controlled their destiny, and they were happy with the life choices they made.

I first saw successful people when I first became a banker out of college. I saw the well dressed, charismatic bankers walking around in expensive suits like they owned the world. They were successful because they portrayed it, and you wanted to be around them.

I thought, what do these people have that I do not have?

They had an "it" factor because they were salespeople, selling the bank's financial products. I called them the "golf & cigar guys". They wined and dined clients, and their job was to make people like them. They had excellent interpersonal skills.

Later in my career, I saw successful people in the private equity business. These people were not selling anything. They were wicked smart, they knew their numbers, and they could problem solve very quickly, outthinking you in a meeting.

I thought these people were successful because they were so smart.

Finally, I saw a real entrepreneurial thinker in a man named Jim Martel. They used to say Jim had ten ideas a day, but only one was good and he had to have people around him to tell him which one was the good one. The people following Jim did not have any ideas, but they were happy to be the number two person. From Jim, I learned ideas and vision could equal success.

So, as I was putting my career together, I used these examples to outline success:

1. **Personal interaction:** For me, it became credibility. Doing what you say you were going to do vs. being a back slapper.

2. **Knowing the facts:** Understand the numbers and the issues, and preparation for those discussions became critical.

3. **Vision:** Having ideas I could put on paper, then be able to verbalize, and making these ideas so compelling that others would want to follow me and those ideas.

For me, those were vital components of success. For you or your son, they may be different.

But as you can see, it's not money, it's about being impactful and intentional. This goes back to clarity and doing what you love.

Now that you and your son have an idea of his dreams of success let's look at how others have achieved their success. Successful people have several personality traits in common, features that allow them to communicate their dreams and motivate others to follow their vision.

Below are many of the traits of successful people. As you read them, have your son consider how they apply to him. By using this book, you will be able to help him more fully develop these traits. For now, a simple check of yes or no can get you and your son thinking about which qualities your son has already and which ones he needs to cultivate further.

Key Success Traits

1. **They have a vision**: Successful people have visions or dreams of their success and reflect on it every day. These are ideas of what they want their lives to look be. They write down their vision and craft goals and action steps to support it.

    Do you have a dream? YES [ ] NO [ ]

2. **They write down their goals:** Successful people write down their goals and put them where they can see them every day, like on a mirror or desk.

    Do you have written goals? YES [ ] NO [ ]

3. **They understand communication and expectation**: Successful people know most problems arise from poor communication, which leads to false expectations. They know how to communicate clearly and let other people know what to expect.

    Do you understand how to communicate clearly?
    YES [ ] NO [ ]

    Do you understand how to set up expectations for others?
    YES [ ] NO [ ]

4. **They take responsibility**: Successful people take responsibility for their decisions and actions. They do not make excuses, and they do not blame others.
Do you take responsibility for your actions? YES [ ] NO [ ]

5. **They are dependable:** Successful people can be depended on by others. They follow through on promises. They live by a basic life rule: "Do what you say you are going to do."

Can people depend on you? YES [ ] NO [ ]

6. **They have a problem-solving attitude**: Successful people find solutions to their problems; unsuccessful people complain about their problems.

Do you seek out solutions even when things are difficult?
YES [ ] NO [ ]

7. **They reflect on their decision making**: Successful people understand their life is a collection of the decisions they make. They think about the proper choices and what they did right, and they think harder about the decisions that did not work out and ask why.

Do you reflect on the decisions you have made?
YES [ ] NO [ ]

8. **They don't fear failure**: Successful people know there is no failure, only delayed success. Each fault can be turned into a learning experience to make yourself better.

Do you treat failure as an opportunity to grow? YES [ ] NO [ ]

9.   **They have a plan**: Successful people always have a plan. They know those who fail to plan, plan to fail.

Do you create plans when faced with new challenges?
YES [ ] NO [ ]

10. **They have initiative**: Successful people are organized and are continually taking action. They don't wait for others to tell them what to do. They are always thinking about the next step, the next goal, the next project.

Do you take the initiative to act before waiting to be told?
YES [ ] NO [ ]

11. **They keep a positive mental attitude**: Successful people maintain a positive approach to life. When they get depressed or negative, they recognize it and accept it as part of the journey. They either take a time out, or they have mental techniques to change their mood.

Do you know how to stay positive? YES [ ] NO [ ]

12. **They are self-disciplined**: Successful people are highly disciplined. They do the hard things first and find a path forward despite challenges or obstacles. They understand life is about delayed gratification.

Do you do the hard things first and wait for the good stuff?
YES [ ] NO [ ]

13. **They are critical thinkers**: Successful people get all the facts possible then they make thoughtful decisions.

Do you collect all the facts before making a decision?
YES [ ] NO [ ]

14. **They accept adversity**: Successful people know trouble is inevitable, and things will get in the way of their plans. They accept it. They learn, improve, and keep moving forward.

When things get hard, do you keep going? YES [ ] NO [ ]

15. **They push themselves outside of their comfort zone**: Successful people continuously push themselves into new ventures outside of their comfort zone. They know they accomplish the most when stretching themselves beyond what feels comfortable.

Do you do new things you are not comfortable doing?
YES [ ] NO [ ]

Achieving success is about understanding where you are now, understanding where you want to be, and following through on a plan to get you there. Keep the traits of successful people in mind as you and your son shape his goals and get ready for his journey.

Which traits of success do you need to work on? Look at the items for which you answered "no." List them below under the "Traits To Work On" section. How will you address these traits? Enter your action steps into the right-hand column.

Traits to Work On	**Action Steps**
Ex: Fearing failure	1. Recognize when you're afraid of failing.
	2. Think about what failure would mean. If I don't get an "A" on a test, is that really failure?
	3. Reframe your thinking to improve and learn, rather than live in fear.
1.	
2.	
3.	
4.	

Part II

The Success Roadmap

Chapter 3

Relationships

It Starts with You: Personality and Likability

To be successful, you need to be likable to other people. Remarkably few people ever achieved their goals by sitting in their basement, not interacting with others.

Being likable is becoming a lost art as the younger generation relies on text and video chat instead of true human interaction. Your two most essential skills in life will be your ability to connect and interact with others, and then your ability to deliver results once you win someone's confidence.

So how do you develop a winning personality? It's not hard if you adopt the six basic principles outlined below. You don't always have to have them all, even if you have half, you will be very far ahead.

I have a good friend Vince, and while he is not always successful in the monetary sense, he is very successful in people liking him. When you meet Vince, he is always positive, no matter how his day was going. He always met you with a smile. He would ask about you and would never brag or talk about himself. He is the most reliable person I know. It's obvious when talking with him that he is a man of high integrity.

Every man should seek to achieve this in their own way. There is no success in life without having a high degree of integrity. It's not something you can say, others will know it from your actions.

I have another friend, David, who has made a lot of money, so successful in that way, but he is difficult to be around. He is always trying to one-up your accomplishments. If you did something, he did it twice and bigger and better. It's hard to be around David because he is trying to make himself feel good by making you feel bad about yourself. This is a losing attitude. Don't be David. While he has made a lot of money, people don't like being around him, and no one really trusts him.

In short, people want to be with, work with, and partner with people who make them feel good and who are honest and reliable. It's the most natural path to success.

Now that your son has written down his goals, these mile markers are tips and exercises on how best to achieve his personal goals and reach his dreams in all areas of his life. The quality of his relationships is an essential ingredient in achieving success. Creating strong relationships where people begin to follow him and his vision is the key to leadership; it takes excellent communication skills, interpersonal skills, and integrity. In the end, it's about being "likable" and respected.

Key traits for developing good relationships:

1. **Have a positive mental attitude and outlook**: You project happiness to people around you. Staying positive keeps others positive.

2. **Be friendly and smile**: Show you are easy to talk to and that you want to speak to others. Being open and inviting will make others feel more comfortable.

3. **Be relevant to others:** Show interest in other people's interests. Being meaningful and showing genuine interest in others will create a stronger bond.

4. **Have empathy for others:** This is the ability to recognize and relate to other people's feelings. Paying attention to others' emotions will show you care about how they are doing.

5. **Be honest and have the utmost personal integrity:** You can gain the trust of others by being honest and straightforward. Honesty and integrity are vital in establishing lasting relationships.

6. **Be reliable:** Being someone people can count on will separate you from most others. Follow this one "life motto," and you will separate yourself from 99% of the crowd. **"Do what you say you are going to do."**

Positive Emotions/Characteristics

Ex. Happy, trusting, caring

Negative Emotions/Characteristics

Ex. Angry, jealous, overly competitive

Interacting With Others

No one can achieve their goals alone; it will take a "team" of other people throughout your life. These will be a combination of close friends, business acquaintances, or people you transact with one time. It does not matter as the same basic principles apply.

You must get others to like you and trust you. If you follow the outline in this chapter, you will become an expert on interacting with others. When this happens, good things will follow.

One of the most successful people I know is named Gene. He has built multiple businesses, he has a following of investors, and people want him to be their mentor. Gene has many of the traits outlined in this chapter.

Even though he has been very successful, he does not act like it. He has no flashy clothes or fancy watches, etc. He is disarming and comes across as one of the guys. He listens to you and makes your problems seem important to him. He has combined excellent personal skills. This is the most potent combination of skills you can have.

I remember one time when I was having a business problem, and I had a crucial meeting, and he understood the importance of the meeting. He asked me to write out a script and practice how the meeting could go. I walked him through the writing and the key points and themes I needed to get across. He then responded like he was the person I would be negotiating with. He taught me how to look ahead at every interaction and define "victory" in my mind. This taught me to make sure I knew the outcome I wanted before I started any meeting. If you know exactly where you want to end up, you will feel tremendous power and will more easily achieve your goals.

It was through Gene that I learned the importance of scripting out important conversations.

For some, creating new relationships is difficult and does not come natural. Here are some key actions that your son can use to help with new key relationships.

When meeting someone for the first time:

1. Look them in the eye and say hello: Tell them your name and repeat their name.

2. Smile, be nice, be pleasant: Show an interest in the other person's interests. Ask questions about the things they like; this will help make them like you.

Follow these tips when you are building relationships:

1. **Be an excellent communicator**: To have strong relationships, everyone has to communicate. Sometimes people don't know what to say. To be an excellent communicator, you must first be a good listener. **Ask questions, and encourage people to talk about themselves.**

2. **Make other people feel important:** Do this by showing you are both interested in and impressed with what they have done. Be sure to compliment them where appropriate. This will show you care and understand. Don't turn a conversation into a competition by trying to prove you are better at something. If they are better at something than you are, try to learn from them.

3. **Create connection points:** When interacting with others, find connection points, common links like school, sports, hobbies, and so on.

4. **Remember other people's names**: Use the other person's name at the time you meet. A good "trick" to help learn the other person's name is to repeat their name a few times during the conversation.

Meetings and phone calls - follow these tips before important phone calls or meetings:

1. Build a conversation script before important phone calls or meetings: Write down how you want the conversation to go. Write down the key points you wish to cover then practice that conversation out loud until you are confident of your approach.

2. Know what victory is: Before any meeting or awkward conversation, think about what you want as an outcome. Say to yourself before a meeting or a phone call: I want to achieve "this" from the meeting or call. Always know the result you want.

These tips will allow you to enhance your connections and build better relationships. A key component to your success will be a reliable and ever-growing network of friends and business associates. Ultimately your success in life depends on how you interact with others. Will others listen to you? Will they follow you? Can you present your ideas, so others are willing to take action around your ideas?

A strong network is critical for your long term success.

Have your son give an example of how he has used or are using connection points to interact with others. Identifying these connection points can make conversation easier.

People In Your Life

Connection Points

Ex. Baseball Coach

Ask the coach who he thinks are the best pitchers of all time

Ex. Science Teacher

Ask what they think was the greatest scientific achievement of the last 20 years

Questions to Prepare For Your Conversations

- What do you consider victory or the goal of the conversation?

- What does the other person believe victory is or their goal of the conversation?

- What are the areas you will agree upon?

- What are the areas you most likely won't agree upon?

- How can you use the areas you will agree upon to make progress on those areas you do not agree upon?

- What are you willing to give up or compromise on to get what you want?

- What will be an acceptable compromise from the other person?

Things to avoid when talking to other people:

1. **Talking about yourself** - Unless the other person asks, don't start talking too much about all the things you have done. It will sound like bragging.

2. **Interrupting -** Let people talk and finish speaking. Only speak when there is an opening to speak. The other person will give you a chance – wait for it.

3. **Speaking poorly about others behind their backs** - Successful people talk mostly about ideas, dreams, and goals and how to achieve them. They tend not to speak negatively about people.

4. **Enjoying the misfortune of others** - This is likely a sign of an unhappy, insecure person. Be happy for the success of others, and communicate your encouragement and support in conversation.

5. **Failing to try to understand the other person's position or reasons** - If you disagree with them, don't get upset, ask them to help you understand their point of view.

6. **Reacting too quickly to what other people say -** Be quick to think, slow to respond. Don't be afraid of a little silence. When you answer too fast or too emotionally, you may regret it.

Things I should consider avoiding in conversations

Ex: Laughing when someone makes a mistake.

1.

2.

3.

Friendships – Building Your Inner Circle

Your friends are important and say a lot about who you are. Picking your friends is a big decision; they are the base of your network. They are your "inner circle". They provide you advice, and they will share your success and failures. Everyone must have a strong inner circle. These include friends, parents, teachers, mentors, and role models.

Good friends have many strong traits. People who will be a positive influence on you and will be a valuable part of your inner circle tend to have the following characteristics:

1) They talk about things they are interested in, not other people.
2) They share common interests.
3) They have strong values.
4) They accept you and support you.

If your friends don't support you, don't be afraid to move on and get new friends. It is difficult, but well worth it.

Build a great inner circle.

Trait 1. Example: Trustworthy and loyal

Trait 2.

Trait 3.

Trait 4.

Trait 1. Example: Good listener and understanding

Trait 2.

Trait 3.

Trait 4.

Now that you understand what you can look for in a friend and what you offer as a friend think about whether the friends closest to you are helping you meet your goals.

Communicate your dreams and your goals to your friends. Maybe they can provide you, even more support and opportunities to grow.

When Other People Get Angry – What to Do

When you are a leader of a group or organization, someone is always upset about something. Allowing people to be upset and blow off steam and even criticize you directly is a crucial skillset you will need.

One time, my CFO, Paul, met with me and was visibly upset. I asked him what was wrong? He started in at me, saying my strategy was wrong, that he felt cheated, and his remarks went from business to personal attacks.

As he was talking, I was thinking about how I would handle this. I did not stop or interrupt him. I let him finish. I asked him when he stopped if he was done, and he said yes.

I told him some of his points were correct and quickly admitted I was wrong. On some of his points, I had to explain my thinking again that led to the decision. To do this, I apologized for him taking it personally, as that was not my intent. Then I stopped talking. There was an awkward silence, but that was okay. (You need to appreciate the power of silence vs. talking.)

While he didn't like the outcome, he respected it and was able to get things off his chest. The fact that he was allowed to confront me without repercussion personally, actually made me a stronger leader in his eyes.

The key in these situations is to let the other person do more of the talking and find places to admit you are wrong, while still getting to your desired outcome. The other person will feel better about you and the situation.

Conflict is unavoidable. When people get angry, these action steps will keep you from getting involved in a negative conversation.

1. **Let the other person finish what he or she is saying.**
   - Don't interrupt.
   - Show respect for the other person's opinion.
   - When they are done talking, ask them if they are done and if there is anything else they would like to say.

2. **If you are wrong, admit it quickly, and move on.**

3. **Agree on what you can.** Find all the points you agree on first. Talk through those. Save all the points you disagree on until the end. The list will be shorter than you think.

4. **Do more listening than talking**. A key strategy to resolving conflict is to let the other side do most of the talking. You will find out their true problems and motivations. Then you will have more information for how you want to respond.

5. **Know when to stop talking.** Once the other person agrees, stop talking. Most people don't know when to take yes for an answer.

The one who talks the loudest doesn't always win. During moments of conflict, the most thoughtful person wins.

Person who is angry and why

Ways to keep the conversation positive

Ex. Mom is angry because I came home late

Let her fully explain why she is angry, find points to agree on

Telling Someone Something They Don't Want to Hear

1. There will always be times when you have to tell someone something they do not want to hear. While no one likes to deliver bad news, below are some tips on how to tell someone something they don't want to hear. Begin your conversation in a friendly way.

2. Don't call attention to the other person's mistakes directly (don't rub his or her face in it).

3. Talk about your mistakes before criticizing theirs.

4. Ask a question rather than issuing a command. For instance, "What if we did this?" or "You might want to try this." No one likes to be told what to do and take orders.

5. Let the other person save face, don't make him or her feel like an idiot. Talk in terms of improvement and solutions, not in terms of mistakes or failure.

Situation

Ex. Need to tell science partner to do his or her share of the work.

Situation

How to Tell Them

Ex. Talk about what needs to be done and what will happen if it doesn't get done. Ask how your partner will help get things done.

How to Tell Them

What to Avoid

Ex. Avoid pointing out partner's mistakes or failures.

What to Avoid

Chapter 4

Time Management

What Is Time Management?

I was first introduced to real-time management at 26. I was working at Sovereign Bank, and a woman a few years older than me was talking about how great her time management system was and how she was so much more productive with it. At this point in my career, I was using a yellow pad and sticky notes. She introduced me to a system called Time Design. I still use it today.

There are many systems. They can be paper-based or electronic, but they have the same essential elements.

The key to all these systems is to get things out of your head and in to your time management system. This gives you clarity and peace of mind.

Time management is a key tool in achieving success.

If you do this, you will see a huge increase in productivity. The goal is a clear mind to solve problems and do things instead of a cluttered mind with things you are supposed to do.

Getting and using a time management system changed my life.

Now that you have your dreams (overall vision), goals, and an understanding of relationships, let us discuss how to put these things to work. We all have a limited amount of time to get things done.

Time management is the ability to break down years, months, weeks, and hours, then understand what you need to get done within those timeframes. Always be looking ahead.

Those without effective time management frequently:

- Forget things
- Miss deadlines

- Hand in work late
- Feel rushed

In his book, *The Seven Habits of Highly Effective People,* time-management expert Steven Covey puts time and tasks into four categories:

1. Urgent and important – must be done now
   - Crises
   - Big problems
   - Deadlines approaching

2. Not urgent but important
   - Preparing for a group project at school
   - Studying for a test
   - Building relationships

3. Urgent but not important
   - Interruptions like your phone ringing

4. Not urgent, not important
   - Watching TV
   - Playing video games or playing on your phone

These are good baselines to work with. The trick is to have a system, spend time with your system, and know what you're doing when and why.

Having your time organized is one of the biggest keys to your lifetime of success.

Things to Accomplish in the Next Year

Ex. Run a 7-minute mile

Things to Accomplish in the Next Month

Ex. Research and set up a training plan

Estimate the number of hours it will take to do the work in the next month. Having a logical estimate will lead to more practical time management. List all of the steps necessary to achieve the goal then add up the total number of hours it will take.

Task	Estimated Time in Hours
Ex. Set up a training regimen	3 hours

Total Hours:

Creating a System

Time management starts with a system for planning and tracking your time. Your son's success in reaching his dreams is determined by his day-to-day activities and how well he sticks to his plan.

Your system should include some of the following:
- Year: What needs to get done this year (this is tied to goals)
- Month: What needs to get done this month
- Week: What needs to get done this week
- Day: What needs to get done today

Help your son choose a method to track your progress and help keep you accountable when dealing with:
- Deadlines
- Report due dates
- Meetings
- Practices

Always work backward from the deadline.

Each month:
Review what needs to happen in the upcoming month.

Each week:
Every Sunday, review what needs to happen that week.

Each day:
Each evening review what you need to get done the next day. Then block off time on your calendar for you to do specific things. Think of this as blocking off time to meet with yourself.

Example:

7:00 am	School
2:00 pm	Out of school
2:30 pm	Home: Study 2 hours for chemistry exam
4:30 pm	Break
5:00 pm	Read book for English
6:00 pm	Dinner
7:00 pm	Finish math assignment
7:30 pm	Plan for the next day and review the upcoming week
8:00pm	Relax (ex. watch TV)
9:30pm	Bed

Your tracking method can be:

- Phone/Computer
- Calendar
- Meetings with a parent or teacher

The key is to help your son pick a tracking method that works best for him and stay with it.

Things to Accomplish This Week

Monday: Ex. Math assignment, 2 mile run, music practice

Tuesday:

Wednesday:

Thursday:

Friday:

Saturday:

Sunday:

Chapter 5

Decision Making

The Two Voices in Your Head – We All Have Them

How to use them to obtain what you want

I remember learning about two voices in my head when I was young. I was 13 years old, and I was trying out for a baseball team in the next city over from mine. I did not know anyone on that team or in that league. I just saw an ad for an open tryout.

I got on my bike, loaded with my baseball gear, and road five miles to the ball field.

I remember stopping about 100 yards away. I could see all the parents and kids, but they could not see me.

I was scared and turned my bike around.

There was a voice in my head telling me, "Go home" "you're not good enough - you don't know anyone - you don't belong here."

Then another voice said, "Stay - if you don't try you will never know" "stop listening to that negative voice."

I turned my bike back around and rode to the field. I was met by the organizer, who made me feel welcome.

I did the tryout and I made the team.

In the first game, I went 4-4 with two doubles and 4 RBI's. My name was mentioned in the local paper. I became a solid part of the team and played with that team for 3 more years.

If I had listened to the negative voice, I would not have had such a positive experience and would never know what I missed.

Two voices are normal, but knowing when to shut the negative voice down is the key to success.

Everyone has two voices in their head. This is natural and normal. Once you understand it's normal to have these two voices, it's your job to shut out Voice One and consistently listen to Voice Two.

- Voice One: The negative voice - You cannot do this. You will fail and bad things will happen.
- Voice Two: The positive voice - You can do it. You're amazing,

Once you understand these voices will always be there, you can use positive self-talk to manage them.

For example, when you arrive at a gathering, and you don't know anyone, Voice One will say "you don't belong here" and "you are going to look stupid." You need to recognize this and shut out Voice One. Use Voice Two to say, "this party will be fun" and "I'm going to meet great people."

Positive self-talk can help you overcome the fear of failure.

Constantly ask yourself:

"What would I do if I knew I could not fail?"

The answer is typically go after your goals and passions.

True success comes when you push yourself outside your comfort zone, shut down voice one and follow your passions.

How Voice One Influenced You

Ex. I thought I would fail, and I became afraid to audition for the solo in the school play.

Outcome

I didn't audition. And so I didn't get the part.

How Voice Two Influenced You

Ex. I told myself if I do poorly on the college entrance exam. I can study more and retake it.

Outcome

I had more confidence and scored high on the test.

How to Make Good Decisions

In order to be successful in life, you will have to make good decisions. Every successful person makes decisions constantly. Very successful people are thoughtful, methodical and have a decision-making process that they follow. While others will just say yes or no, or will "go with their gut" or instinct right away.

There is no question that a thoughtful decision process leads to the best outcomes.

I have a saying: **Life is merely a string of decisions you have made that you are now living with.**

When we started our current real estate finance business, we were leaving the safety of a large corporate employer. Striking out on your own is always scary and requires good decision making. We gave ourselves six months to get this new venture off the ground.

To succeed, we needed a partner and we knew exactly what we were looking for:

- Financial backing
- Market presence
- A need or fit within their business plan

After six months of meetings, the choice came down to two companies. They could not have been more different. One was a large insurance company and one was a New York private equity fund. The insurance company was easy to deal with and they were full of nice people. The private equity firm was full of smart people, the smartest, but it was more of a competitive environment. But they were also highly focused and were on a mission to succeed, while the insurance company valued family life and long vacations.

I knew it would be "easier" working with the insurance company, but I was afraid they would be slow to respond to the urgency I had as a young entrepreneur.

We thought about the pros and cons for a long time. My partner and I put their names up on a white board and analyzed each one. We ran financial models of what we thought each one would look like.

In the end, we decided to go with the private equity firm. We understood the risks, but as a young company, we wanted to be with the smartest, most driven people we could find. We knew we were giving up "partner character" for this decision, but we got comfortable with that, and would now be playing with the best in the business.

In the end, it was the right decision. They pushed us very hard and we learned a great deal in a short time period. We did more business with them than we would have done with the insurance company. But it was always difficult to prove ourselves and they made us work very hard to show why our investment decisions were right. That vigorous process made us even better.

The partnership only lasted a year, but we proved to ourselves and to others in the business that we could hold our own with the best in the industry. In the end, that was the validation we needed that led to bigger and better accomplishments.

Once you have transitioned your dreams into goals, and your goals have action steps, you must start making decisions around those action steps.

Decisions don't just happen. They need to be thoughtful, and good decisions need to be intentional. Below are five steps for good decision making that will keep your goals on track.

1. **Know where you want to end up** - Know what you want, and know what victory is. Know what you want to achieve.

2. **Seek clarity in your goals.** Know what you need to achieve each of your goals.

3. **Be proactive.** Don't get "frozen" when you have to make a decision. Sometimes a wrong decision is better than no decision. You must always be moving forward.

4. **Think critically:**
   a. Get all the facts
   b. Understand how the facts work together
   c. Make your decisions with the best facts available at that time.

5. **Link your decision back to your goals.** Does this decision help you achieve your goals? If yes, do it. If no, think about whether or not you should do it.

Before you make any big decision, make sure you are very clear about what you want. If you have "total clarity", decision making becomes much more comfortable.

The Decision You Made	Did you end up where you wanted to be?	Did you take action right away?	Did you get all the facts first?
Ex. I will try out for the team.	Yes	Yes	Yes

Chapter 6

Success Techniques

Creating a Great Life – Rules for Everyday Life

It is easy to fall back to bad habits. And if you do, achieving your dreams will be difficult.

Keep these things in mind. They will be vital to staying on track.

Eight Rules for Everyday Life

1. **A positive mental attitude.** Keep smiling and be positive. Good things happen to you if you remain optimistic.

2. **The power of your subconscious.** Solve your problems and achieve your goals by using the power of your mind. Your subconscious mind is powerful and always working. You can get closer to achieving what you want by keeping your goals visibly posted around you. If your subconscious is aware of your goals, you will consciously recognize more opportunities.

3. **Accept adversity.** Roadblocks may get in the way of you achieving your goals; misfortune will happen. Embrace it as an opportunity to improve. You have to learn from adversity.
   Ask yourself:
   - What went wrong?
   - Why did it go wrong?
   - What can I do differently next time?
   - Do not get emotional about it. Acceptance is a big part of success. Accept the adversity and keep pursuing your goals.

4. **See it and say it.** Once you know what you want, write it down in a simple phrase or sentence. Put it on your mirror. Read it every day. Say it out loud. Mirror Goals are a very powerful technique for achieving what you want (we will talk about them more in the next chapter).

5. **Be proactive.** Keep moving forward all the time, even in small steps. Achievement and success are a process, and they do not come all at once. Once you know what you want, start building out the action steps to get there. You must keep focused on the future, not the past.

6. **Have clarity.** Success requires clarity. Clarity is the confidence of knowing what you want at all times. Clarity will bring you a sense of calm and a sense of mission at the same time. **You must have a clear picture in your mind of what you want.** Once you do, you can start the process to achieve these things.

7. **Understand the risk.** Before you make any decision, understand the possible outcomes. What good can happen? What bad can happen? Understanding and managing risk is a key success component.

8. **Learn from other people's successes.** Learn from those who have already accomplished what you want. Model their processes and replicate their success, then build upon it. You can achieve great things by learning from others.

By using the Eight Rules for Everyday Life, which ones does your son need to work on the most? Write them down below. Identifying the rules most relevant to him will help you set relevant goals.

Rule to Work On

Ex. Accept adversity

How Will You Work on This?

Ask myself what went wrong
and try to fix it instead of
beating myself up.

Fear: The Big Success Killer

Techniques to Recognize and Conquer Fear

Remember, success is not a straight line. Remind your son to keep these things in mind to work through adversity:

Fear: Fear kills all dreams and takes away potential greatness. It is a very destructive emotion. You need to recognize it and learn how to battle it. When you experience fear, take a time out and think clearly about the situation at hand.

How to beat fear: Fear is usually brought to your attention by Voice One (mentioned in Chapter 5). The voice in your head that is telling you all the things that could go wrong. You must recognize that this is natural. To beat fear, you need to go to Voice Two and remind yourself of all the positive things you want. You need to have Voice Two shut down Voice One. Use Voice Two to speak positive outcomes and to push fear out of your mind.

Linkage: When using Voice Two to shut down Voice One, we use a concept called linkage. The key to linkage is tying a pleasurable outcome to your fear. For example, "If I study an extra hour, I will do better on the test." This links to better grades, a better college, and a better career.

When did you give in to fear or self-doubt?	**How could you have worked through it?**
Ex. I stayed home sick to skip my test.	I could have linked having a stress-free weekend to finishing the test on time.

Part III

Your Ongoing Journey to Success

Chapter 7

Setting Your Goals and Designing Your Life

Goals Versus Dreams

There is a big difference between dreams and goals. Dreams are easy, and they don't require accountability. Goals, on the other hand, are hard. They require action steps and progress.

I was always goal-oriented. I'm not sure why. Maybe because things did not come easy to me, and I learned early on that goals were stepping stones to things I wanted. In short, goals lead me to my dreams.

I would always have a notebook containing my goals. The goals were all different, such as school, baseball, friends/social life, hobbies. Later in life, it was about jobs, careers, graduate school, and money. I had specific action steps and deadlines for those action steps. That process held me accountable to myself.

A friend of mine had dreams, big dreams about being a movie star. He would talk about these dreams all the time, but he did not have any goals. He would talk about going to Hollywood or New York with the character he created and how he would make it big one day.

While I was working on my goals, and taking action, he was just talking about his dreams.

I made steady progress in my life. My career developed, I got married. I had a son. I started a business and I sold a business. This was all very intentional. They were all my goals. They were written down with action steps and timelines.

My friend, on the other hand, never became an actor. He still talks about his dream, his character, and how it "could have been". He has a nice life, but never fulfilled what he wanted because he never transitioned his dream into goals.

You need dreams, big dreams. Everything is possible when you are young. Your options narrow the older you get. You must take these dreams and then turn them into goals. Once you have goals, you must break down into the action steps needed to get to your goal.

This will turn your dreams into reality. Without this method, you will just become one of those people who talk about "what could have been". Don't be one of those people.

What is the difference between a goal and a dream?

Dreaming is a big picture. It is the final place you want to be in any aspect of your life. It is what you see in your "mind's eye". It is how you see yourself being successful based on your definition of success. To reach your dreams, you have to set goals. To achieve your goals, you must have immediate action steps.

- A goal is a stepping stone to get to your bigger dreams. You may have to accomplish multiple objectives to achieve your dream. Every purpose should have action steps that you can work on every day.

Once you know the dream (or vision) for each part of your life, you can build your goals to achieve those dreams. By completing your goals, you will ultimately reach your dreams.

Regularly review your goals and keep the following in mind:

- **Success is a long road.**
  Success doesn't come quickly. If it did, everyone would be successful. Be persistent, stick to it, and don't be afraid to ask for help.

- **Success is a marathon, not a sprint.**

  Be consistent, work hard each day. Be careful not to burn out. Give your mind and body a rest when you are frustrated.

- **Always think about and review your dreams and goals.**

  Check-in and ask yourself if you are getting closer to your dreams. Regularly review your goals and change them as needed and as you get closer to your dreams.

- **Your dreams may change.**

  Life changes and the things you want may change, too.
  It is okay to alter your goals as things in your life evolve.

The Art of Goals and Goal Setting

Setting goals can be a complicated process. Most people don't do it or have difficulty doing it, and yet it is essential for achieving success.

Your goals are a roadmap and stepping stones to your dreams.

Your goals will guide your decision making, will allow you to see opportunities, and will allow you to live a life with purpose.

To set reasonable goals, you will need to:

1. Know what you want
2. Set goals to achieve what you want
3. Create action steps for each goal
4. Take action on those steps
5. Set deadlines (to measure your success)

Don't be afraid to set goals that may seem challenging to achieve. That is how leaders get things done.

Put your goals in writing.

Your goal plan has to be in writing. People who have written goals are much more dedicated and will eventually achieve their dreams and their definition of success. People who do not commit their goals to writing are only "hoping" to achieve their dreams. They are simply dreamers and not doers.

Setting your goals to ensure they achieve your dreams.

A goal is measurable. It either happened, or it did not. Getting 1400 on the SAT is a quantifiable goal. Doing well on the SAT is not a measurable goal. That is a hope in which successful people rely on goals and action steps. Unsuccessful people rely on hope and luck.

When you think of goals, think of the first few letters of the alphabet: A, B, C, and D. Each letter represents a goal building block:

- **A**ction-oriented
  - o What immediate action can be taken now?
  - o What are the future action steps needed to achieve the goal?
- **B**ased on what you truly want
  - o Is this goal for yourself or someone else? You will be more passionate about the goals you truly want.
  - o Define an outcome and go after it.
- **C**ommunicated
  - o Tell others your goals so they can hold you accountable.
  - o Make it clear to others what you want.
- **D**ocumented
  - o Put your goals in writing where you can see them daily.
  - o Monitor the progress of your goals.
  - o Change them over time, but keep a record of where you were and where you are now.

Here's an example:

Dream: To become a successful college student.

Goal: Achieve a score of 1400 on the SAT

Immediate action step: Each night, study both algebra and biology for an hour each.

Future action step: Take geometry and physiology next semester.

The Success Plan

The Success Plan will be your guide/playbook for your future. Just like a football team has a playbook, this will be yours. Once you have done it one time, you will just have to adjust it from time to time.

The Success Plan is the culmination of this book. It is the reason you read this book. It's your system to make sure you are on the right track. It's the outline where you will make adjustments. It's your "Life Plan".

I have broken down the plan into the **Big Six Life Categories**. You can use these or add some or take some away. For each of these areas, you need a vision or dream of what you want. Once you have that, you turn the dream to goals, then action steps.

One of my son's dreams growing up was to play on the varsity baseball team. This was a dream from an early age. So, when he was still in middle school, we had this as a goal. But a goal without action steps is meaningless. So we built out a weight training routine, a diet plan, and a practice plan.

We spent two years of "training" for the tryout day. When that day came, he did well, and he made the team. The satisfaction that comes with accomplishing a goal through hard work (action steps) is a feeling you want your son to have at an early age.

This is the most important section of the book. Develop a Success Plan, and work with your son, and you will develop a great man.

Now that your son understands the difference between dreams and goals, it's time to build his Success Plan. His Success Plan will bring everything together in one place. Keep it close and review it often.

The Success Plan will have six sections about each of the **Big Six Life Categories** introduced in Chapter 2.

1. School
2. Sports/activities
3. Relationships
4. Hobbies/passions
5. Health
6. Job/career

On a piece of notebook paper, have him write out all six sections of his Success Plan, one part for each of the Big Six Life Categories. Each section of the Success Plan will consist of the elements below:

BIG SIX LIFE CATEGORIES:

Dream:
Goal:
Immediate Action Step:
Future Action Step:
Key Due Date:

Example Success Plan Sections

SCHOOL
Dream: To become a college student at a prestigious university.
Goal: Achieve a score of 1400 on the SAT
Immediate Action Step: Each night, study both algebra and biology for an hour each.
Future Action Step: Take geometry and physiology next semester.
Key Due Date: January 1st

HOBBIES/PASSIONS
Dream: Turn my hobby into a career, become a professional musician.
Goal: Get booked for a paying gig.
Immediate Action Step: Practice my instrument for 1 hour each night.
Future Action Step: Speak to 4 restaurant owners and offer to play.
Key Due Date: June 15th

SCHOOL

Dream:

Goal:

Immediate Action Step:

Future Action Step:

Key Due Date:

SPORTS/ACTIVITIES

Dream:

Goal:

Immediate Action Step:

Future Action Step:

Key Due Date:

RELATIONSHIPS

Dream:

Goal:

Immediate Action Step:

Future Action Step:

Key Due Date:

HOBBIES/PASSIONS:

Dream:

Goal:

Immediate Action Step:

Future Action Step:

Key Due Date:

HEALTH

Dream:

Goal:

Immediate Action Step:

Future Action Step:

Key Due Date:

JOB/CAREER

Dream:

Goal:

Immediate Action Step:

Future Action Step:

Key Due Date:

Condensing Your Son's Success Plan to One Page

Now go back and review your son's Success Plan. Help him continue to refine it. Then have him put it on one page so that he can post it to his bedroom wall and keep it with him at all times.

Look at the example that follows, then have your son complete his one-page Success Plan.

Example Success Plan

The following is a sample of what your son's one-page Success Plan might look.

	School	Sports/ Activities	Relationships	Hobbies/ Passions	Health	Job/career
Vision	Get into college of choice	Professional musician	Supportive and helpful	Have a world-class comic book collection	Injury-free	Be financially secure
Goal	1400 on the SAT	Perform in front of an audience at a paying gig.	Support my friends when they need me.	Get the top 3 comic books from each manufacturer.	Build muscle.	Get a high paying job.
Immediate Action Steps	Every night, study algebra and biology for one hour each..	Practice my instrument for 1 hour each night.	Make a calendar of my closest friends' significant events.	Go to a flea market every week and look for comic books.	Weight lift three times a week.	Create a resume.
Future Action Steps	Take geometry and physiology next semester.	Speak to a coffee shop and restaurant managers to look for paying gigs.	Be there for every big event to show my support.	Do on-going research on how much the collection is worth and who may be willing to buy it.	Work with friends and coaches to improve the lifting technique.	Apply for three jobs.
Key Due Date	Jan.1, 2022	Sep. 1, 2021	Sep. 1, 2022	March 15, 2023	Feb. 1, 2021	Feb. 1, 2021

Exercise:

Have your son fill in his own Success Plan. Downloadable worksheets are available online at www.BoysToMenGuide.com. Then have him entering his goals, action steps, and deadlines.

	School	Sports/ Activities	Relationships	Hobbies/ Passions	Health	Job/career	Other
Vision							
Goal							
Immediate Action Steps							
Future Action Steps							
Key Due Date							

Mirror Goals

Congratulations! This is the final exercise! In the last two sections, your son has identified the parts of his dreams, his goals, and his action steps.

I have always been a big user and believer in mirror goals. They remind you daily of the most important outcomes to your current plan, and they stay in your mind all day. This is one of the most important traits I passed down to my son, which has helped him achieve the things that were important to him.

This bullet point summary of the goal-setting that you have done is so powerful but underused.

An example of my son's high school senior goals:

- Get a 1300 or better on the SAT

- Get into one of his top 3 schools

- Save $1,500 for college

An example of my goals as I was growing a business:

- Raise a third round of funding

- Get total company assets under management to $500 million

- Recapitalize the company over the next 12 months

These goals should be changed and continuously updated, but your son should always have a 3x5 card of his top goals on his bedroom mirror. It will reinforce goals, action steps, and drive him toward the success he wants.

He now has a detailed plan that he will keep at home as well as a condensed one-page version that he can post so he can see it daily and have with him at all times. Together, these make up his Success Plan.

Mirror Goals are another easy way to make sure he is continuously working toward his dreams and goals.

Mirror Goals allow your subconscious mind to think about achieving your goals, even when you are not working on them. Your subconscious mind is potent and your Mirror Goals will unleash that power.

Have your son take a 3x5 card (like the example on the next page) and write down one key phrase, action step, or key goal that relates to each of his dreams and sections of his Success Plan. It should be his primary goal that relates to his desires or overall vision. It should be a critical goal that is the next stepping stone to his dreams - something measurable that he will know is done or not.

Then have him put the 3x5 card on his bathroom mirror and read it out loud twice a day (both morning and night).

You will be amazed and pleasantly surprised how much faster your goals are achieved if you let your subconscious mind do a lot of the work for you.

Example Mirror Goal Card

1. 1400 on the SAT

2. Perform music live

3. Form a band

Putting Your Plan into Action

To have the best chance to achieve the Success Plan, your son will need to look at his Mirror Goals twice a day, when he wakes up in the morning and when he goes to bed. When he looks at them, he should say them out loud. This will allow his subconscious mind to start working on his dreams and goals. He will now be working toward them even while he sleeps!

Review your Success Plan every week to check your progress and ensure you are taking the appropriate actions.

- Dreams
- Goals
- Action steps

Don't be afraid to change your goals or modify your action steps. Things change, and you need to change your plan accordingly.

By reviewing your Success Plan every week, you can be confident that you are on track. If you change your goals (all in pursuit of your dreams and overall vision) be sure to change your Mirror Goals as well.

Remember, the road to your son's success will be a windy, bumpy one. Your son's goals will keep him focused and on track as he achieves each part of his dreams and ultimately achieves the life he wants. If he does that, he will have arrived at his definition of real success.

Additional Notes

Additional Notes

Additional Notes

Additional Notes

Best Wishes

My dear friend and fellow parent,

Congratulations on finishing this book. By taking the initiative to read the book, spend valuable time with your son, engage him in the exercises, and reflect on his goals, he is now well on his way to designing and creating the life he wants.

But your journey doesn't stop here. The dreams, desires, and ambitions that you've identified as you worked through this book together will change, and that's okay. This book serves as a lifetime tool, one you can use over and over again as your son grows and matures. Return to it often. I suggest four times a year to check on your son's progress and make any modifications needed. This is now his lifetime road map to success. Feel free to adjust it over time, but continually come back to the guard rails as required.

Success is not a straight line. There will be good and bad days, and there will be setbacks. But if your son has a plan and goals, the setbacks will not seem as bad. His goals will give you strength and help you make any course corrections along the way.

The one big key to a lifetime of success is to keep moving forward. Take action. Remember to believe in your son and yourself as a parent. Use the methods I've outlined here, and believe in the plan. Your son's current plan may not work, and you may need a new plan, but his goals will be the driving force to keep him focused.

I wrote this book for my son with one goal in mind: to give him the tools to be a great person. I am excited to pass these tools on to you. I know this book will change your son's life if he lets it.

I wish you a lifetime of success and happiness. You now have the roadmap to get there.

Best wishes,
Jay Rollins

For downloads and worksheets visit www.BoysToMenGuide.com

About the Author

Jay Rollins is a father, entrepreneur, real estate expert, and has been a featured speaker and guest lecturer at numerous real estate conferences, colleges, and universities. He is also the author of *Commercial Real Estate Uncovered,* a guide to success in commercial real estate.

Long before graduating from George Washington University with an MBA in Finance, Jay Rollins knew real estate. His father, a real estate entrepreneur, exposed him to the art of the deal from an early age.

As CEO of his Denver-based finance company, JCR Capital, and with more than 30 years of real estate experience, Rollins has seen it all. With the highs of the 1980s, the crash in the early 1990s, the RTC era, the dot com bust, the run-up in 2005-2006, and subsequent crash in 2008, Rollins has seen real estate fortunes lost, and made again.

Mr. Rollins started his career as a commercial banker with regional lenders in the Washington, D.C. area. He then went on to become a borrower, serving as the Vice President of Finance for a large Washington, D.C. based public homebuilder.

When the 1990s real estate bubble burst, the U.S. government was aggressively closing banks and calling in loans on historically good borrowers, only to sell them to entrepreneurs. Mr. Rollins quickly recognized this was a generational opportunity and established his first venture, Eastern Realty. Eastern purchased distressed loans from the Resolution Trust Corporation (RTC) and savings & loan banks. This venture went on to buy over $400 million of distressed assets over four years.

After selling this company in the mid-1990s, he created a balance sheet lending platform for GMAC commercial mortgage. Starting from scratch, Rollins built a nationwide commercial real estate lending program that financed over $1 billion in loans. In 2006, he founded JCR Capital, a commercial real estate finance company targeting middle-market assets. Today, Jay Rollins is a recognized industry leader and frequent speaker on commercial real estate.

He is best known for calling the top of the commercial market in 2007. Mr. Rollins is a graduate of Virginia Tech with degrees in finance and marketing and received his MBA at George Washington University.

Index